THE SELF-TAUGHT SAXOPHONE PLAYER

A GUIDE FOR UNCORKING SAX-PLAYING
TECHNIQUES

LOUISE LAWRENCE

A Wizwind inspiration

Uptake publications

Taunton. *TA4 2AR*

DEDICATION

For Digger Dee,

a sax player who will never let the grass grow under his feet.

CONTENTS

INTRODUCTION

Why do I squeak?

How can I make my breath last longer?

How can I make a better sound?

These frequently asked questions and many more are answered in *The Self-Taught Saxophone Player*.

This neat little guide offers an original, highly effective and succinct visual approach to quickly mastering the correct basics of saxophone technique. Learning by yourself can feel rather lonely and without a witness to your progress it is all too easy to pick up habits that will limit your progress.

Keep this friendly book on your music stand as a touchstone for all practice sessions and dip into it when you pause for breath.

Rather than replicate the many comprehensive tutor books and online videos already available, this book focuses on the most common issues you are likely to come across along the way. Hopefully you will find the advice contained within these pages interesting and fun.

Why the pictures? Because we all learn differently. An idea put one way can be baffling, put another way can be obvious. I'm a visual learner. If an idea is given to me in picture form, I get it immediately and the message endures. Hopefully my quirky illustrations will act as a trigger, reminding you of the points taught in the text, whether a Bull Frog, a Cathedral or a Puppet.

This is the rough order of things

• Nuts and bolts of the saxophone itself: how best to set it up

• How to get the best sound: control of mouth, body, breath and tongue

• How to manage the instrument: control of fingers and harnessing the brain

• Accessories, trouble-shooting and maintenance

…oh yes and… Back Page – at the back of the book!

Happy playing.

> *'The saxophone is so human. Its tendency is to be rowdy, edgy, talk too loud, bump into people, say the wrong words at the wrong time, but then, you take a breath all the way from the center of the earth and blow. All that heartache is forgiven. All that love we humans carry makes a sweet, deep sound and we fly a little.'* **Joy Harjo**

INSTRUMENT PURCHASE

A BIT OF SAVVY AVOIDS DISAPPOINTMENT

It really *is* advisable to buy from a music shop specialising in woodwind instruments. Why? Because instruments usually come from the factory needing final preparation before re-sale – a job the shop's repairer will do.

Your instrument will come with a warranty, and the shop's repairer will sort out any technical issues. Non-specialist shops often send instruments away to get the job done – which means involving a third party and a frustrating wait for you.

There are plenty of sparkly new instruments available online, but best to be a bit savvy.

Some manufacturers cut corners in construction and/or use inferior quality materials – this will ultimately affect your progress. My instrument technician friends now refuse to work on cheap quality imports because they cannot be made to play well.

Second-hand instruments can be economic and successful if you can get your purchase to a teacher or repairer first. Let

PUTTING THE SAX TOGETHER
THE SAFE WAY

The saxophone is a large instrument and putting it together when you first start can seem a daunting task. Metal can easily dent, keys can bend and reeds can break. Here's a simple way that avoids this from happening. Order is important:

- *Mouthpiece onto Crook*
- *Reed onto Mouthpiece*
- *Crook onto Horn*

This is the best order. If you set up the reed on the mouthpiece and then push the mouthpiece onto the crook, you will most likely dislodge the reed and have to set the position of the reed again, or else damage the reed by manhandling the mouthpiece and reed together.

Mouthpiece onto Crook

Before screwing the mouthpiece onto the crook, take a look at the crook and observe the long, hinged key attached to it. This is the octave key mechanism. This key is easily bent and moved out of alignment, so the best way to avoid this happening is to gently but firmly clasp the thinner end of the crook so that the octave key is held down in a closed position.

Holding crook without damaging octave mechanism

Holding the crook in your left hand with the cork end uppermost, screw on the mouthpiece about halfway down the cork, checking that the mouthpiece hole is lined up with the raised crease on the lower side of the crook. Both holes should now be facing you. Ensure cork is well greased. (see p. 88).

Mouthpiece and crook holes facing

Reed onto Mouthpiece

Select a reed and suck it three times, each time drawing it from the mouth slowly (like a lollipop stick).

With the crook still held in your left hand and mouthpiece hole facing you, place the reed, flat side down, against the mouthpiece. Hold the base of the reed (the shiny part) with the left thumb. With the right hand, adjust the reed so it's in line at the sides with just a thumbnail of black showing at the top.

Slide the ligature over the top of the mouthpiece, being careful not to catch the tip of the reed. Pull the ligature right down so that it is sitting on the shiny section of the reed, making sure you are not obscuring the curve of the scraped down section, otherwise you will restrict its flexibility.

Reed inline - ligature avoiding bottom curve of reed

The screws should be facing you. You can now screw them up with your right hand. (Single screw ligatures, just screw at the back on the right. Material ones often have holes in the fabric at the front – just be sure to get the holes absolutely central over the reed).

Screw securely, bottom screw, then top – do not force. Pop the reed cap back on for now.

Crook onto Horn

First ensure you are wearing your sling.

If the saxophone feels large and unwieldy at first, you can manage it this way. Raise the body of the instrument out of the case by the narrower neck end. Rather than lift it out of the case entirely, you can keep it resting on the soft interior and twist it so that the bell is turned away from you.

Clip the sling onto the sax. Check the top opening of the horn, and you will see a small rod-shaped key that projects up vertically.

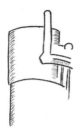

Rod key sticks up vertically from horn

This is another key liable to bending, so the angle at which you attach the crook is important. Holding the top of the horn in the left hand, and the crook in your right hand (observing correct handling of the octave key mechanism), you can now slide the crook into place. Keep the mouthpiece pointing towards you and then you will avoid bending the vertical key on the horn. Line the vertical key so it's in line with that raised crease on the lower side of the crook – it should now be situated around halfway within the loop of the octave key mechanism.

Linking and aligning crook to horn

Lift the complete saxophone out of the case, and with your right thumb under the thumb rest and left hand in place on the finger pad keys, the sling can take up the weight of the instrument. **Never rely on the sling hook clip and let go of the saxophone completely**. Sling hooks can easily break, and the saxophone can swing and get knocked all too easily. If the sling is too long or short to bring the mouthpiece to the right height for you to play, you can always rest the instrument back on the case again to make the necessary adjustments.

When the sling length has been corrected and you are holding the instrument in position, the mouthpiece should comfortably come into line with your mouth ready for you to blow. Now you can take the reed cap off and the reed should easily come into place on your bottom lip.

If needed, you can make very slight twisting adjustments to the mouthpiece and crook if needed.

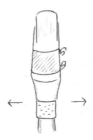

Mouthpiece twist

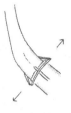

Crook twist

Always *adjust the instrument position to you, rather than adjusting your position to the instrument* and then you will avoid unnecessary strain to your neck and upper body.

'Don't play the saxophone. Let it play you.' **Charlie Parker**

3

MOUTHPIECE POSITIONING - EMBOUCHURE

SKIN OF LIP

Skin of lip

Controlling the sound you make is hugely dependent on how much mouthpiece you use and where the reed sits on the lower lip (the embouchure).

Try this:

Place the index finger on your lower lip.Gently push all the fleshy red section of the lower lip over the lower teeth – *check on how this feels* - this is too much bottom lip

Now place the index finger on the lower lip and repeat the exercise, but this time just pushing in *half* the fleshy red section of your lower lip – this feels like just the skin of the bottom lip – *check on how this feels* - <u>this is correct</u>.

You have already set up the reed on the mouthpiece and it is connected to the crook. So holding the crook in your right hand, reed facing you, place the thumb-nail of your left-hand against the side of the mouthpiece slightly beyond a third of the way down between the tip of the reed and the top of the ligature, just above where the mouthpiece curves away from the reed.

Thumb guide - where the mouthpiece curves away from the reed

With just the 'skin' of the lip over the teeth, slide the mouthpiece in until your thumb is against your chin. Place your teeth on top of the mouthpiece. Adjust and adapt the positioning slightly until it feels comfortable. The angle between the mouthpiece and the chin needs to be somewhere between 70 to 80 degrees.

Here it is helpful to visualise a tennis court. Imagine the tennis net pulled between the sturdy metal posts. Draw your lips back very slightly as if you were drawing up the slack on

the tennis net from either end. The corners of your mouth remain sturdy like those metal posts.

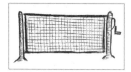

Drawing up slack on a tennis net

A large volume of air is needed to play the saxophone. The chapter on diaphragm breathing explains how to take in sufficient air and control that flow of air out and down the saxophone, but the suggestions below will get you going for now.

Breathe heavily though the mouthpiece and crook as if breathing steam on a window.

Steamy window breath

Keeping the 'steamy window' concept in mind, direct your steamy air down the saxophone as if blowing through a straw. This will give you enough air pressure to get the reed vibrating and produce a sound.

Check in a mirror that your cheeks are not puffed out. Done correctly, you may see slight dimples in your cheeks.

Puffed-out cheeks result in bunching of the bottom lip. The bottom lip muscles control the flexibility of the reed, so it's important the lip muscles can work effectively. Puffing out the cheeks also affects the shape of the cavity inside your mouth and this will affect the sound you produce.

If you have difficulty producing a sound, you could be pulling back your lips too tightly or clamping down on the reed and mouthpiece.

Firstly, just slacken off the lip tension (visualise loosening the tennis net).

Secondly, imagine stifling a yawn. This just opens out the inside of your mouth and throat slightly and will get you to relax the jaw muscles. Shape of the mouth cavity is covered in more detail in Chapter 7 (Controlling the Tone) and Chapter 21 (Tuning).

'After one month with a saxophone shoved in my mouth, my military combatant's enthusiasm disappeared completely. Instead of flying choppers behind enemy lines, I started to fantasise about living in New York, London or Paris.'

Gilad Atzmon

4

POSTURE

FLEXIBLE BUT ROOTED

Breathing needs to be free and unrestricted. Fingers need to be loose and flexible. Aside from discomfort arising from repetitive strain, tensions in neck, shoulders, upper-back and arms can inhibit breathing and swift movement of the fingers, so how you position your body in relation to the saxophone is important. This needs particular consideration because of the weight of the instrument and also the physiology of the individual.

Arms floppy and relaxed - like a puppet with no strings

Before working with the saxophone, you need to be sure shoulders and arms are completely relaxed.

Imagine you are a puppet. The strings holding up your arms have been cut so your arms hang loose by your sides. This concept will help you to avoid tension.

We are now ready to work with the saxophone.

When the weight of the saxophone is taken up by the sling, right thumb under the thumb rest and both hands in position, you will notice the saxophone tilts naturally at a diagonal angle. By pushing the saxophone away from your body with the right thumb, the angle will alter slightly. You can experiment to find an angle that feels most natural to you. Find a position putting least strain on the neck and shoulders. If a comfortable slant means twisting your neck or chin to be in line with the mouthpiece, then you may need to make slight twisting adjustments to the mouthpiece and/or the crook, (Chapter 2).

Some people find it more comfortable to have the sax angle slightly to the right of their body, and some prefer to hold it more centrally in front of the body. Many players claim that the more central position allows them to project a better sound. Maybe this is because the mouthpiece is brought to sit on the lower lip at a more symmetrical angle. It is worth experimenting. You may also find it interesting to check out images of reputable players and make a comparison.

Keep your elbows away from your sides. Legs need to be comfortably straight and feet planted slightly apart.

Allow a slight softness and flexibility in the knees. The knees act in a similar way to the suspension on a car, absorbing any undesired body movement so that it will not impact on the rest of the body.

Softness in knees for suspension

If you are securely attached to the floor, you will feel more in control of yourself and your instrument. Whatever situation you may be playing in, you will feel relaxed and flexible yet firm and grounded.

Flexible and grounded - like a rooted tree

Sitting down

It is a good idea to practice sitting down as well as standing up when you play, and try both positions with a music stand. As with standing, you may need to experiment a bit to find the most comfortable position. The saxophone can be played directly in front with the bell positioned between the knees, or angled to one side with the bell to the right of the knees. Either is fine, so long as you have adjusted the tilt of mouthpiece and crook. If you're playing in a big band, then it's desirable to match the rest of the sax section with the horn to the side. Therefore it would be good to ensure you can play in this position, if needed.

Shoulders, arms and torso position should be as relaxed as if you were standing.

Sitting on the back of the chair will impact on breathing capacity,

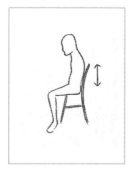

Seated on back of chair - breathing capacity limited

so try to sit towards the forward edge of the chair to optimise the length of the upper body.

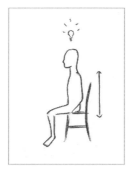

Seated on front of chair - breathing capacity optimised

This forward position will allow more flexibility of posture and, of course, sitting upright will keep you more alert.

5
_____

POSITION OF HANDS AND FINGERS

IT'S ALL ABOUT THE THUMBS

Keep the fingers floppy and relaxed ....

as if drumming the fingers on a table top.

Keep a curved hand position ...

imagine you are gently holding a small, ripe avocado in each hand.

Left Hand:

The left-hand thumb position is important for flexibility and seamless movement between the lower and upper register on the saxophone. Always keep it on the circular thumb rest below the octave key. The thumb needs to be far enough to the left, and far enough down on the thumb rest so the index finger does not catch the palm keys. The left thumb and index finger should form an easy curve around these keys. Further detail on this is covered in Chapter 15 (Palm Keys).

You will need to experiment with this position and tweak it slightly to get the optimum position for the length of your thumb. Check the angle between your thumb and the body of the instrument. Ideally it should be at a 40 to 45 degree angle.

Keep the wrist relaxed and in-line with the left forearm.

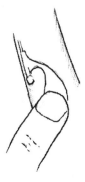

Left thumb position in relation to horn

If you can achieve this position, you will find you can catch the end of the octave key by a very slight bend of the thumb knuckle. You should not need to bend your thumb very far. The shape and placement of the octave key varies from instrument to instrument however. On some models, it can be quite awkwardly placed so the thumb has to be moved some way to the right, across the body of the instrument, in order to reach the key. This is a particular problem for players with smaller hands. In this case you can catch the very corner of the key by twisting the wrist slightly away from you and pivoting on the thumb.

Right Hand:

The position of the right-hand thumb under the thumb rest is important. Too far to the right and it will restrict the flexibility of movement of the right hand; too far to the left and it will feel insecure.

You also need to ensure you do not catch the side keys with the index finger. Ideally it should be between the tip of the thumb and the thumb knuckle (where it bends).

Tweak slightly to get the optimum
position for the length of your thumb.

*Right thumb position
under thumb rest*

'When you play a sax, that saxophone is irreverent. It's noisy; it's a trickster... you cannot hide the saxophone in your hands, so it's a good teacher.'

Joy Harjo

6

DIAPHRAGM BREATHING

PUPPETS AND BALLOONS

Make the most of your air. The diaphragm is like an elasticated rubber sheet resting between the rib cage and the stomach. Used well, you can take in more air and control how you let it out.

How does it feel?

Imagine blowing out candles on a birthday cake (cheeks slightly puffed). Prepare yourself for this – there are 100 candles!

Notice how when you draw breath the shoulders rise and the stomach is pulled in.

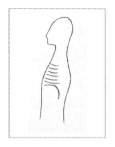

Less air is taken in

Blow the birthday cake air out onto the palm of your hand, and it will feel cold because the air has only been sucked part way into the lungs. The only way to control the speed and strength of that jet of air is by pursing the lips into a whistling shape. This shallow breathing is not making the best use of the diaphragm. Notice also how extra tension is stored in the upper body, shoulders and arms? This will adversely affect posture and flexibility of finger technique.

Now imagine breathing steam on that window pane. Prepare yourself for this – there are four panes!

Steamed up window

Notice how when you draw breath this time, the shoulders stay relaxed and the abdomen extends?

Breathe the window air onto the palm of your hand and it will feel warm because you've taken the air right down to the bottom of your lungs. You can breathe your lungful of air out slowly and steadily, or more quickly in a fast

More air is taken in

'Ha'. This deeper breathing is making good use of the diaphragm. Upper body, shoulders and arms are now relaxed. This will improve posture and flexibility of finger technique.

Exercises to get started

NB: *These exercises are best managed in front of a good sized mirror so you can keep a check on what is happening.*

First of all, we need to get a sense of where the diaphragm is.

To do this, just place a hand on your stomach – somewhere between the bottom of your rib cage and your belly button.

Make three short sniffs in close succession. You will feel your stomach puff up like a balloon.

If you stand side-on to your mirror when you do this, you will see your abdomen extend.

Turn back to face the mirror.

To make best use of the diaphragm, the shoulders should stay in a relaxed position and never become raised. Visualise the puppet, (Chapter 4).

Place your hand back on your stomach and make those three sniffs again – stomach puffing up like a balloon.

Relax, and let the air out. Repeat this exercise a few times.

Now continue with five or six sniffs until your stomach feels fully extended – air sucked down to the bottom of the lungs. Relax and let the air out. Repeat a few times. Keep a check in the mirror – shoulders should not rise, arms floppy and relaxed.

When this feels natural, open your mouth very slightly and:

LET the air *in* – one long swoop - *abdomen extends out.*

LET the air *out - abdomen relaxes back.*

Check in the mirror that the shoulders are not rising up. If they are, go back to the puppet position, arms floppy and relaxed by your sides. Then try the exercise again.

(Just an aside here – the word "let" is more useful than 'breathe' in this exercise. The word 'breathe' usually triggers automatic reverting to default breathing habits. Interestingly, if you were to lie on the floor you would find your stomach fills out when you breathe in, and relaxes as you breathe out).

Before testing this out on your saxophone, we need to convert this warm stream of air from the diaphragm into a controlled jet of fast air, sufficient enough to get the reed vibrating.

You may find it helpful to think of a pressure hose:

The air comes from the diaphragm (the water tank) up through your airway (the hose).....

Air coming up from diaphragm like water through a hose

Your lip musculature (forming your embouchure) directs the air into a fast-streaming controllable jet.

Pressurised jet of air

Now, try this out with your saxophone. Take a long swoop of air into the diaphragm, settle your lips into their embouchure (visualise the tennis net position – posts supporting on eitherside and drawing up the slack in the net) – and now breathe out through the saxophone on a bottom E.

Check in the mirror. Your shoulders should not move.

Test it out

Check how long your bottom E note lasts. You can practise your breathing anywhere, any time. The more you exercise the diaphragm, the longer your bottom E will last, and the more control you will have over the sound that you make.

A positive thought

Learning to use your diaphragm when you breathe will not only benefit your saxophone playing. Diaphragm breathing also reduces the effects of anxiety – a wonderful skill that can be used in your every-day life!

Caution:

If you feel light-headed, just take a break and come back to the exercise later.

> *'The worst waste of breath, next to playing a saxophone, is advising a son.'*
>
> **Kin Hubbard**

7

CONTROLLING THE TONE

TUBES OF SOUND

The concept of the sound you would like to produce on the saxophone can be developed by plenty of listening. You may already be inspired by a particular sax player, or drawn to a particular style of playing. Diversity of tone and style is perhaps more apparent within the sax-playing fraternity than for any other instrumental group.

Here are some factors:

Hardware – the set up

- Make and model of instrument

- Make, model, material and dimensions of mouthpiece

- Make, style and strength of reed

- Make, style, and material of ligature

- (Varied combinations of all the above)

Software – the player

• Musical Influence

• Musical Experience

• Physicality, personality and energy of the individual

• (Varied combinations of all the above)

Software interacting with Hardware

Manipulation of notes – vibrato, lip bends etc.

Quite a substantial list, but one thing is for certain – to secure a good foundation for building your own saxophone voice you need to develop control of lip and diaphragm, and the very best way to do this is to spend time playing long notes.

Choose a favourite low note. Take in air, using your diaphragm. Breathe out through the sax to produce a long steady note. Visualise this as a solid tube of sound. Keep it level – no wavering.

A solid tube of sound

Choose a higher note, and repeat. Choose a lower note, and repeat. Continue doing this – low note, high note, middle note. Prepare for each note by filling the diaphragm. Listen for a level sound remembering to visualise a solid, round, unwavering tube.

When this feels natural and fairly under control, you can consider what is happening *inside* your mouth. The space inside your mouth (the mouth cavity) is your sounding box. You can increase the resonating chamber inside your mouth by opening out the throat slightly and altering the position of the tongue, (more on this in Chapter 21).

Imagine placing a cherry on the back of your tongue while you play your tubes of sound.

Now expand the cherry until it becomes a cathedral – large and spacious.

This should feel similar to stifling a yawn, (Chapter 3).

Cherry on the back of the tongue

Large and spacious cathedral

While you play your long notes, experiment with this concept and listen carefully to the subtle changes in tone. If you practice long notes at the beginning of each practice session, you will be exercising the diaphragm, strengthening your lip muscles and tweaking the shape of the tone chamber inside your mouth to get the very best tone. It's a really good all-round workout. The more time you spend on this, the more control you'll have over the sound you want to create.

If you do this daily, you may think your note tubes are becoming more wavering, or your sound is not improving. This is perfectly normal. Don't be disheartened. You are only becoming more aware and perceptive, which is the surest way to success. You cannot help but improve by spending time on this exercise.

> *'As a horn player, the greatest compliment one can get is when a person comes to you and says, 'I heard this saxophone on the radio the other day and I knew it was you. I don't know the song, but I know it was you on sax.'* **Clarence Clemons**

8

LOWER REGISTER

BULL FROG

Many people struggle to get the lowest notes on the saxophone when they're in the early stages of playing. In some cases, this is because the lips are pulled too taut. If so, you can just loosen the tension (tennis net - Chapter 3). In most cases, though, it is because the air just isn't getting down to the end of the saxophone. The effect you are likely to get is a bubbling sound.

If the saxophone had no bends in it, you would see it is conical in shape. This means that not only is the length of the saxophone becoming longer as you put more keys down, but it is getting wider too.

The air needs to fill the instrument completely for all the notes to speak......

The volume of the saxophone is large. The volume of an alto sax is roughly 9,092 cubic cm. That's equivalent to 16 pints, (19.2 US pints).

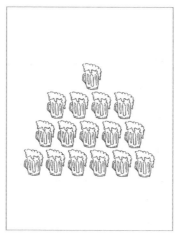

16 pints!

Sax players with mathematical inclinations might enjoy making their own calculations:

Tenor?

Baritone?

Bass?

Contra-Bass?

So to play the alto sax, you need to have 16 pints of air at your disposal and have continued control over that air. You are certainly going to need support from the diaphragm. You may want to re-visit the diaphragm breathing exercises, (Chapter 6).

It's also important you maximise the tone chamber within your mouth for a resonance. Remember, the space inside your mouth can be made larger. Visualise the cherry on the back of the tongue expanding to the large and spacious cathedral, (Chapter 7). This will feel similar to stifling a yawn.

The throat needs to be open and relaxed so the air is not restricted. How does this feel?

Try this

Place the fore-finger and thumb of your right hand gently on either side of the top of your neck – just under your chin. Now try stifling that yawn again. Notice how the finger and thumb are pushed outwards as the upper neck expands.

Visualising a bull frog might help.

Bull frog throat

Here is an exercise for developing tone control down to the lowest notes of the saxophone:

Play a steady one-finger B – solid tube of sound, support from the diaphragm. Keep the note level and make it last as long as your breath will allow. Take the air into the diaphragm and play the B again, slur down to the B♭ and hold it as long as your breath will allow. Take the air into the diaphragm and starting on the Bb, slur on down to the A. All the while, try to match the sound of the note pairs.

The mouth and throat are actually a continuation of the saxophone conical tube, so as you work your way down to the lower notes you need to be aware of the cherry resting on the back of your tongue. It gets larger and larger towards the cathedral.

As the notes become deeper, the cavern in your mouth becomes larger and the bull frog throat expands.

Keep working down to the bottom C, B and finally a full resonant bottom B♭.

Tip

Large interval leaps from higher notes to the very low notes can be particularly challenging. For example an A to a low C. This is because when you play an A, the length of the saxophone tube is short and narrow. When you play a low C, the saxophone tube is much longer and wider. However swiftly you move your fingers for the lower note, there will be a delay in getting enough volume of air to the end of the instrument. Remember to keep the volume of air travelling through the saxophone, (visualise those 16 pints).

Try this

Play the 2-finger A while holding down the C key with the right hand little finger. Now move the other three fingers of the right hand slightly higher off the horn and bring them down with a slapping motion as you move from A to bottom C. The low C should just pop out easily. Experiment with this slapping technique, moving now from a one finger B to low C and then the octave jump from a C to low C. You could then try slapping for low B and Bb. Just keep the C key on, as before, along with the low B key for bottom B or the B^b key, if you want more of a challenge.

One last word on low notes – it's really helpful when attempting your first bottom notes to just let rip and imagine a rich fat fog-horn to get things going. This relaxes everything and can also be good preparation for playing the higher E, F and F$^\sharp$ (see Chapter 10).

*Let rip like a rich fat
fog-horn*

'The saxophone is the embodied spirit of beer.'

Arnold Bennett

9

WRIST TWIST

DOOR HANDLE

The little fingers have the job of operating the heaviest keys at the bottom of the sax. They are not only the weakest fingers, but they are also the shortest, and yet they have the furthest distance to stretch. The wrists are strong and their job is to twist. Using a twisting action will help you move swiftly across the keys at the bottom of the instrument.

Try this

Take the right hand off the sax and hold it out as if you were going to shake hands with a friend. Instead of shaking hands, imagine you are twisting a door knob. Notice how the wrist and forearm move as one.

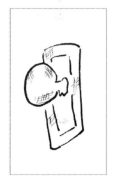

Twisting the door knob

Now play a good rich sounding 6-finger bottom D – a long tube of sound, air supported from the diaphragm. Now move the little finger of the right hand down to the C key, take it off and move it onto the E^b key. Play over and over.

Now try sliding directly from the C to the E^b key. Try moving backwards and forwards.

Left wrist

Take the left hand off the sax and remind yourself of the door knob twist action, but this time working with the left hand and forearm. Now place your left thumb back on the instrument being careful to position it correctly under the thumb rest, (Chapter 5).

Play a good rich sounding bottom C – a long tube of sound, air supported from the diaphragm. Next, move the little finger of the left hand down to the B^b key. By using the twisting action you'll find you can depress the B^b with the tip of the little finger. If you have small hands, the side of the finger can be used rather than the tip. Now come back to C and move the tip of the finger down to the B$^\natural$ key. Continue the movement – off for C, down to B^b, off for C and down to B$^\natural$.

Now try sliding directly from the B♭ to the B ♮ , backwards and forwards. The rollers between the keys are there to enable this sliding movement between the lower notes. For players with small hands, manage this movement by keeping the tip of the finger on the B ♮ key and use the door twist action to bring the side of the little finger down onto the B♭ key, pivoting on the thumb of the left hand.

The left C ♯ key uses a slightly different wrist action. Try sliding from the low B directly to the C ♯ key and you'll notice you can only move backwards and forwards by raising and lowering the wrist. As with the octave key, the shape and positioning of the left hand little finger keys and rollers can vary, so it's just a question of experimenting with what works for you on your instrument.

These wrist exercises are a good way of checking your thumbs are in the optimum position for your span width and finger length. Be aware of any feelings of strain and tension, and tweak your thumb positions accordingly.

NB: *An instrument technician can lighten the spring action for you if you are finding the lower keys heavy and stiff to operate, (Chapter 25).*

10

HIGHER REGISTER
STRONG AND SECURE

If your left thumb is positioned correctly on the thumb rest, the upper register notes can be reached by bending the thumb very slightly, or pivoting on the thumb to depress the octave key, (Chapter 5). Remember to keep the thumb resting on the thumb rest at all times and ensure you are using the pivoting action. Some people jump the thumb off and on the octave key, which makes this register change much harder.

A strong, rich and secure sound in the lower register is an excellent anchor on which to build top notes.

Try the following exercise, and experiment to find the most effective and comfortable position for your thumb.

Play a bottom D (a rich tube of sound), do not slacken off the air flow - now just **bend or pivot** the thumb to get a top D. Play a rich bottom E and slur up to top E, then F and continue working up to G, A, B and top C.

The exercise we used for strengthening the low notes in the previous chapter also works really well for securing the higher notes. Just invert it. Start with playing a 6-finger upper register D – a controlled tube of sound, support from the diaphragm. Next, start with the D again, but move on up to D♯ and hold the note. Now start on D♯ and move on up to E. Just continue upwards in semitones, always holding the 2nd note of each pair.

Keeping the air flowing whilst slurring up in semi-tones

Remember to keep the air pressure up whilst tweaking embouchure and tone chamber to create a level round sound.

If notes squawk, stay low pitched, or don't sound at all in the upper register, then check out the points below:

Insufficient air pressure

Many people are scared of squeaking on the higher notes, so they use less air. The reed needs to vibrate faster for the higher notes to sound. If you don't keep the pressure of air going through the saxophone, the reed will stop vibrating and there will be no sound. Either that, or the reed will vibrate too slowly, and you will just make a groaning sound.

Solution:

Visualise the solid tube of sound and use plenty of air support from the diaphragm. Don't slacken off.

Too much tension

Sometimes the top notes won't sound at all. If you feel tense about playing higher, it is easy to start biting. This presses the reed against the tip of the mouthpiece and closes up the gap – the reed becomes restricted and the air can't get through to make it vibrate.

Solution:

Firstly, try slackening off the pressure. Visualise slackening off the tennis net. If this doesn't work, try putting a tiny bit more mouthpiece in your mouth, just to open things up. When you feel more secure, just keep the air pressure up, but ease the mouthpiece out again to a comfortable position that allows the top sounds to come through. You can make a rounder tone by imagining the cherry sitting on the back of your tongue.

Not enough tension

To keep the reed vibrating at a faster pitch, the bottom lip needs to be pulled slightly tauter.

Solution:

Visualise pulling up the slack on the tennis net so it is tauter at either end. Keep the tube of sound solid, supporting it from the diaphragm.

The reed is too soft

The softer the reed, the more flexible it is. Flexibility in a reed is important, but a reed that is too soft can be pushed so close to the mouthpiece tip that it restricts the air flow when you tighten the embouchure.

Acid eats through reed

Reeds also become more pliable with age (acid in the saliva eats through the wood), so consider how long ago you changed your reed.

Solution:

Put on a new reed. If you can't do this until later, then a good quick fix to keep you going in situ is to adjust the reed higher so it's in line with the top of the mouthpiece with no 'thumb nail' of black showing. This really is **only** a short-term fix, until you have an opportunity to pop a new one on.

If the problem persists, then you may be ready to move onto a stronger reed. The likelihood is that your lip muscles are strengthening and developing. If you are on a strength 1.5 (a soft, pliable and easy reed to get started on), then move up to a 2. The higher the number, the more dense the reed (Chapter 26) for more on reeds.

NB: *It is also important that the throat remains relaxed and open, the space in the mouth cavity is not too restricted by the tongue, and the lips are not pulled too tight. This all sounds rather technical, but you can do this easily just by listening to the sound that you are making.*

Try some long, sustained notes in the upper register. Visualise tubes of round unrestricted sound, listening all the time. While you breathe through these notes, you will be subconsciously tweaking the position of your lips, jaw, throat and tongue to create the best warm round tone – matching musculature feel to sound. This is an innate skill – after all, it is how we learn to speak.

'If you like an instrument that sings, play the saxophone. At its best it's like the human voice.'

Stan Getz

11

B TO C

SEE-SAW

Switching from B to C fingering is surprisingly difficult to manage neatly in the early days of playing the sax – try this slurred and you will probably hear a blip in between the two notes. What usually happens is this: the middle finger comes down before the index finger comes up. This is because it takes less energy to drop a finger than to raise it.

So if you were to do this movement slurred in slow motion, you would hear the note in between:

B to C becomes B A C

The same thing happens when moving from C to B. The index finger drops down before the middle finger raises:

C to B becomes C A B

This movement happens so frequently that, if you don't work a neat switch into your technique, any slurred playing will always sound messy.

The challenge:

Middle finger drops *as* index finger rises

Index drops *as* middle finger rises

Think of a see-saw

The seesaw switch

45

This pesky little corner of technique is easily achievable. Go slowly enough so you can think about what your fingers are doing, but ensure the finger switch action itself is very swift and slick. Always do this slurred and then you can really hear whether you have eradicated that irksome middle note.

B......switch......C......switch......B

Do this every day at the beginning of your practice and when you can do it neatly with no blip, just build up speed.

A thought

It is easy to become impatient and move on too fast, fingers moving rapidly onwards before the brain has planned what the fingers actually need to do. If you can slow things down enough so the brain has time to work out what the co-ordination challenge is, then you are likely to get things right first time. It is all about setting up the correct motor memory.

Set up good habits right at the start, and you won't have to waste hours of time correcting yourself further down the line. For more on this check out Chapter 18.

12

THE BIS KEY

TO BIS OR NOT TO BIS

If you are working with a saxophone tutor book, then you will have discovered the **bis key.** If there are flats in the key signature, you can just slide the left-hand index finger slightly down so it covers the bis key as well as the B $\natural$ key and all the B's will automatically come out as B^b.

Why use the bis key

In writing this book, I have really enjoyed discussing various aspects of technique with other sax players, and the subject of the bis key has instigated some healthy debate. From the players I've spoken to, it appears that flute players doubling on sax are comfortable using it because the concept is the same as using the B^b thumb key on the flute. Clarinet players doubling on the sax can manage perfectly well without using it because they have already worked the side key mechanism into their technique. Interestingly, one clarinet-sax doubler told me he finds the bis key constrains free movement between B^b and B $\natural$ when improvising.

Another sax player, who does not play clarinet, told me he would find it impossible to improvise at speed in a flat key without using the bis key, and he rarely uses the side key. On the basis of these various discussions, my conclusion is that players who come to the sax at the outset happily use the bis key because it is just a key on the saxophone to be learnt and used like any other. For the purposes of this book, therefore, I've taken the following approach. Learn all the fingerings for B^b and develop a technique that allows you to use any of them effortlessly. This will give you an ideal starting point from which you can adapt to whatever technical needs you encounter along the way.

Working the bis key into your technique

At first, this can feel really awkward, and it is tempting to avoid using it altogether, but stick with it. It will allow you to play more swiftly in flat keys in the long run.

The use of the side key and 1/1 fingerings for B^b are covered in the next chapter. Meanwhile, here are some exercises you can use to work the bis key into your technique. Run through them at the beginning of each practice session. Progress to an F major scale, then move to a piece with B^b in the key signature. If you do this every day for a week, it should feel comfortable and automatic.

This exercise will be most useful to you slurred, then you will be able to hear if your fingers are moving together. With the B to C action, remember to move slowly at first to avoid that pesky blip, (Chapter 11).

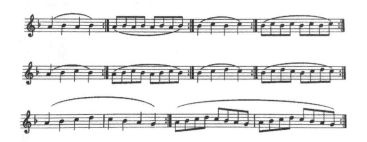

'I understood that if I wanted to work, the saxophone was the main instrument. The clarinet was what we call a double.'

Lee Konitz

13

B FLAT FINGERINGS

MAPPING IT OUT

Plan ahead – when to switch, and when to use the side-key.

If the music switches between B♭ and B♮, then you may need to switch your index finger from the bis key to B♮.

A thought

It is possible just to roll between the bis key and the B♮ key, and there are excellent players who do this, but if you are just starting out, then you are building your technique from scratch. Why not take advantage of the complete key system as Adolphe Sax intended.

Let's work with just the index finger switch for now, from the bis key position to B♮. We can look at the alternatives later.

It is a good idea to plan out your finger movements in advance. If you don't do this (the lazy option), you are likely to embed repeated mistakes.

Try this:

Switching the index between B♮ and B♭:

Asterisk the music at the beginning of the piece with whichever B you are starting with. Move on to where there is a change. Seek out an opportunity to move your index finger before the change. This will be either when you are playing a C or C♯ because you are not using your index finger, or during a rest when you have time. Asterisk the music with the change of fingering. Continue on in this way, marking out where you need to switch.

Marking the index finger switches

Just a note here - in the context of this chapter, I am referring to the side key as an alternative to B flat, but in general, it is best to think of the side key fingering as A♯ rather that B♭. Here is the reason. If there are no flats in the key signature, then you would have your finger on the B♮ key and just use the side key for A♯ as needed, whether it's in the key signature or is an accidental in the music. The movement would be therefore be side key A♯ to index finger B♮.

There are times however when you are in a flat key and encounter a B♮ as an accidental and you need to move between B♭ and B♮ quickly with no opportunity to switch the index finger over. This is where it may be easier to keep the index on the B♮ key throughout and just use the side-key for passages with B♭.

You don't need to asterisk, just write 'sk' above the B♭ where needed.

Marking where to use the side key

Using the $^1/1$ finger B♭:

If you have your index finger on B ♮ and you have to move to Bb from an E or an F, you can use the $^1/1$ fingering (left and right index fingers), in which case you can just pop $^1/1$ above the B♭ and not change the index finger.

Marking where to use the 1/1 fingering

When you first start a piece, you may need to try different Bb options. Find the ones that work best, then map out your piece, marking the fingerings and changes. That way, you will be playing all the accidentals correctly and will avoid embedding mistakes. Make best use of your practice time and progress will be quicker, (Chapter 18).

14

FINGER STRETCHING

MOORHEN TOES

A certain amount of finger strength is needed to play the sax, more so than the clarinet or flute because the keys are larger. Stronger springs are needed to keep the pads open and closed. All the fingers need to be able to move independently from each other, and the fourth finger is weaker than the index and middle finger. The little finger is the weakest and yet it has the most demanding work of shifting the largest and most heavily sprung keys at the bottom of the horn. Also, you need a fair stretch to reach the little finger keys.

Here is an exercise that will improve independent co-ordination and stretch for each finger.

Try this for co-ordination.

First, hold up your left hand – palm facing away – as if saying 'Stop!' Keep your fingers closed – now stretch your fingers open – now closed.

Now try this:

1. Move just your little finger away from the other fingers and back.

2. Now, keeping little and ring fingers together, stretch them away from the other fingers, and back again.

Little finger and middle finger stretch

3. Now move little, ring and middle fingers out and back.

4. Now move just the thumb out and back.

Index finger and thumb stretch

Repeat the whole process with the right hand.

Now try the whole process with both hands at the same time – you'll find co-ordination is easier.

Try this for greater stretch

This exercise can be done under a tea-table when bored. Separate the little finger of your left hand from the rest of the hand by stretching it across your knee – try again with your little and ring finger together. Repeat with your right hand.

Visualise the stretched claws of a moorhen and make your fingers do the same.

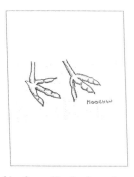

Stretching fingers like the claws of a moorhen

15

PALM KEYS

ANCHORED AND SECURE

Palm keys (left hand)

There are two things to consider here:

1.Managing the keywork

2.Creating the sound

Key-work

The height and position of the palm keys[1] vary between makes and models of saxophone as does the size, shape and positioning of the octave key.

Moving onto the palm keys can feel awkward and unnatural at first, but consider the following four points and you will soon master this aspect of technique:

- Anchoring
- Palm key risers
- Finger Placement
- Wrist Movement

Anchoring on the right thumb

In order to play top D, D♯, E and F, all the fingers need to be raised from their keys, which leaves the bulk of the saxophone resting on just the two thumbs and the bottom lip. This can feel really insecure, and the instrument can then tend to rock alarmingly when you try to depress the left-hand palm keys. The important thing is to ensure you keep the **fingers close to the instrument at all times** .

The other thing you can do is to push the saxophone forward slightly with the right thumb. This will position it more firmly on the lower lip and give you more anchored support.

Thumbs give anchored support

Palm Risers

As mentioned earlier, the palm key positioning will vary between saxophone makes and models, and you may find it is difficult to manage the top note fingerings easily. You can easily adjust the height of the palm keys by buying a set of palm key risers. These are small rubber sleeves you can just slide over one or more of the palm keys to position them slightly higher. If attaining the optimum position for your hand shape is still a problem, then an instrument technician can usually adjust the positioning for you.

Fingers Placement

For the first palm key – D, use the ball knuckle of the index finger.

For the second palm key – D$^\sharp$, use the lower section of the index finger.

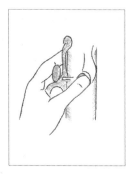

Left hand thumb position around palm keys

For the third palm key – F (when played with the top right key), use the lower section of the middle finger.

Wrist Movement

Dropping the **left wrist** slightly brings the weight of the hand and fore-arm down against the springing action of the palm keys.

Creating the sound

To get started, just enjoy a big 'fog horn' blast on a top D – the note should just pop out. Have another blast and hold the note for longer. Third time around keep the air going and slur on to D ♯ and E. Another attempt and you should be able to slur on further to the top F. The sound won't be sophisticated and mellow, but it will give you a sense of how those notes sound and how they feel.

Moving on to getting a good secure tone, means revisiting some long note practice – visualising those tubes of sound. The slurred semi-tone exercise from Chapter 10 is useful here, but this time starting from top C.

As you slur up in note pairs, remember to maintain the air pressure from the diaphragm. Keep listening so you can adjust the tautness of your lips (tennis net), adjust your tone chamber (between cherry and cathedral) and keep your throat open and relaxed (bull frog).

---

1. *Footnote*
   The German company, Keilwerth, have designed a saxophone with adjustable palm keys. Reviews are mixed, but you can check these out if considering a purchase.

16

TONGUING

TINY HAMMER

Tonguing is the technique of separating one note from the next with the tongue. Most beginners stop and start the note by blowing HOO HOO HOO, or opening and closing the throat, creating an OO OO OO sound.

Saxophone tonguing can be more challenging for some than others, depending on your tongue shape and the way you pronounce words, but it is worth working on. A correct tonguing technique will produce a clear beginning to each note and allow you to play more quickly in the long run.

Try this: (whisper, no vocal chords):

OO OO OO (Throat opens and closes)

THOO THOO THOO (tongue flicks between teeth)

TOO TOO TOO (tip of tongue touches roof of mouth lightly)

DOO DOO DOO (area just behind the tip of the tongue touches roof of mouth with a slightly heavier action)

DOO DOO DOO, TOO TOO TOO or somewhere between the two will work for you.

Now try this:

Get a solid tube of sound going on a nice easy note. Bring in the Doo or Too action. The tongue acts like a tiny little hammer hitting the reed and separating the notes....

chopping up that tube of sound into segments – separate

notes.

Tongue acts like a tiny hammer

Every time the tongue hits the reed, it stops it vibrating. As long as you keep the tube of air going, the reed will vibrate again when the tongue moves away from the reed. The crucial thing is to keep that tube of air going as you tongue.

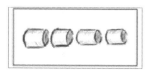

Chopped up tubes of sound

The tongue should hit the reed just behind the very tip.

You need to experiment to find a position that feels most natural for you. The length, shape and musculature of the tongue is likely to determine this.

If this is all too tricky, try single notes – HOOD HOOD HOOD or HOOT HOOT HOOT. Next move to continuous sounds: HOODOODOO or HOOTOOTOO.

When you can do this, progress to DOODOODOO or TOOTOOTOO.

Hoot

NB: *you are now starting the process with your tongue on the reed, so you will feel the pressure of air behind the tongue before the sound is emitted.*

Once the tonguing technique starts to come together for you, it's a question of listening and experimenting to get the clearest sound, minimising the sound the tongue makes hitting the reed. Aim for more note sound and less tonguing sound.

Practise these exercises regularly and you will find the tongue muscles will quickly firm up and the effect will be more subtle and 'clean'. If you visualise the chopped-up tube of sound, the gaps between the sections of sound are getting smaller.

Keep the tongue action soft and gentle, yet positive and precise so the note can continue between strikes, unimpeded by too much heavy tongue.

Imagine a taut washing line (your note tube) with tiny pegs (your tongue strikes). The peg takes up a minute section of

the space on the line, and is so small and light that the line continues with minimal interruption.

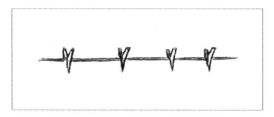

Tongues strikes, like the pegs on a washing line - small and light causing minimal interruption to the sound

NB: *The jaw should not move. The embouchure should not alter. The only thing that moves is the tongue. As the tongue is inside the mouth, there should be no outward evidence of tonguing happening.*

17

SCALES

WHY BOTHER

Why play Scales?

Because scales are the quickest way to learn all the most common finger moves we use in playing music.

Why don't people like playing them?

Because most people get frustrated. They spend ages playing them over and over to get them right, and then when they come back to them later, they go wrong again.

Why does this happen?

Every time a scale goes wrong, your fingers are learning the wrong pattern. If you play the scale over and over, getting it wrong, then you are training your fingers to play a wrong finger pattern – implanting an incorrect motor memory.

Playing a scale wrong is therefore actually worse than not playing a scale at all!

Why are wrong notes unsettling to hear?

Hearing a different sound to the one you are expecting can be an uncomfortable experience.

Different sound to the one you were expecting

Solution

When learning a scale for the first time, play it so... so....slowly that you cannot possibly go wrong. It is best to read it from some kind of notation to start off with. Be sure to read the note and know what the fingering is for that note *before* your fingers move there. It is tempting to let the fingers take off and do their own thing.

If you do play a wrong note, correct it – go back to the beginning of the scale and play only as far as the offending note, but finish on the corrected note this time. *Stop*. Play from the beginning again.

Do this three times and you will have re-trained your fingers so that they get it right next time.

When you feel more secure with your scale, be content to play slowly and steadily. Imagine an elderly person plodding upstairs.

Each stair the same space from the last

You can upgrade to a more youthful jog when you are feeling even more confident.

18

HOW TO PLAY TRICKY BITS

HARNESSING THE BRAIN

Memorising is a valuable tool. By looking away from the music, you can really think about what your fingers are doing and train them quickly to do what you want.

Try this:

Circle the bit you can't play. If this is a whole line of notes, play slowly and work out which notes are the most difficult to move between. Narrow it down to the most challenging three notes, or maybe even just two. Play these notes very slowly from the music three times. Memorise these notes and play them again while looking at a blank wall.

You have now trained your fingers into the right finger pattern. Go back to looking at the music and add in *either* the previous note, *or* the note following, so you now have four notes.

Repeat the process with these four notes, playing from the page three times and then from memory three times.

Continue the process, adding in notes, one by one.

Messy blips

If you have tried this tactic but things still sound messy, remember the issue of the pesky blip when moving from B to C, (Chapter 11). Take each pair of notes in the phrase and listen carefully as you move between them. Check your fingers are moving together. If they move up or down at different times, then you will hear an extra note in between. Work out which finger is moving up or down last. Work slowly so that you can make that sluggish finger to move up or down first.

Now play the whole phrase and get a tad angry with the sluggish note. It will come out correctly because you are paying it extra attention and therefore anticipating it in advance.

G# and D#

Slurring note pairs G# /A, and D# / E will need particular attention. Firstly because two fingers are moving simultaneously, and secondly because in both cases the little finger is operating a sprung key, (Chapter 9). It is easy to adjust the tension on the springs supporting the G# and D# keys if you find these heavy or stiff to operate, (Chapter 25).

Repeating wrong notes

If you keep playing a wrong note in the same place, don't keep playing it wrong – you will be working the wrong fingering into your technique. Go slowly enough from the beginning of the phrase to get the offending note correct. Then repeat three times ending on the **correct** note.

Remember – motor memory – training fingers to do what you want every time.

Keep a check on the state of your brain

This way of working is rewarding, but very intense, so there will come a point when you'll feel tired and things start to fall apart. Maybe change to a different type of practice, now.

Play through something easy you enjoy, or walk away and do something entirely different. Your brain will still be mulling over the niggly problem. When you come back to it next time, you should find, surprisingly, that the awkward section is a lot easier.

> *'I've played every instrument you could possibly think of for 10 minutes. So I'm mediocre at everything.*
>
> *I can play drums, guitar, piano, violin, saxophone, clarinet, flute... Just not well.'*
>
> **Kat Dennings**

19

PRACTICE ROUTINE
WATCH TV

Little and often is best - You are likely to progress more quickly with just a few minutes each day than exhausting yourself with a three-hour session at the weekend.

Keep the saxophone accessible - invest in a saxophone stand. Keep the saxophone out on a stand rather than packed away in a case. Playing a tricky bit of technique while the kettle's boiling, or a few scales while waiting for a phone call is a sure way to save time and move your playing on quickly.

Have a routine. Playing long notes is the best way to start. Get control of your breathing and embouchure. *Rich tubes of sound.*

Next, scales and finger exercises – get control of fingers.

Then tricky sections of pieces (whilst the mind is still fresh).

Lastly, whatever you fancy.

Vary the tasks. If you are bored with long notes, just do a couple, then move onto something else. If you struggle with a scale or a tricky bit of music, don't keep going beyond the

point of weariness or frustration – move on to playing
something for fun.

Always try to bring in something utterly new – try new ways of
doing things: new finger exercises and routines, new music.

Keep inspired and fresh - Listen to other players and recordings,
keep yourself open to new ideas.

Have specific targets to work towards – a "performance" can be as
understated as playing a tune to a friend. Aspirations to
improve technique can be as humble as being able to play
smoothly from one tricky note to another.

Take a break. If your concentration flags, do something entirely
different – watch TV, go for a walk – whatever – and
amazingly enough, when you come back later – you may well
find the niggle you were struggling with has suddenly
become easier.....your brain has been working on it while
you were away from the saxophone altogether!

Take a break - give the brain a rest

'*Play difficult and interesting things. If you play boring things, you
risk losing your appetite. Saxophone can be tedious with too much of
the same.*' **Steve Lacy**

20

READING MUSIC FLUENTLY

EYE HOPPING

If you listen to a young child learning to read, they hesitate between each word:

The.......cat.....sat.......on.......the.......mat.

Big gaps

If you listen to an adult reading the same sentence, the words blend together:

Thecatsatonthemat.

No gaps

Try reading the very first sentence on this page – the one in bold italic. Now read it again, but this time read it out loud. When you say the word 'listen', notice which word your eyes are focussed upon... probably on the word 'young' or 'child'.

This is because we scan ahead with our eyes – and of course reading then becomes fluent. In the same way, *music* will sound more fluent if you can read ahead.

Eye hopping

TIP

Rather than resting your eyes on the longer notes when you play them, use the time to read ahead to the next note. You can use this strategy when you get to a rest, a breathing place or the end of a line.

Consciously make yourself do this, and eventually you will find yourself reading ahead on the shorter notes, too. You'll continue to develop until you find yourself scanning ahead many notes at a time as you play.

21

TUNING

KEEPING WARM AND AWARE

One of the wonderful joys of playing sax is the ability to manipulate pitch with ease. Lip slurs and vibrato lend the instrument its idiosyncratic vocal character, techniques to consider when the basics of tone control are in place. However, such flexibility means that you have to be particularly aware and pro-active to keep the instrument in tune. There are various things to consider.

Tuning etiquette

Altering your pitch to play in tune with others is really important. However adept your playing, you won't gain popularity votes if you don't pitch in with fellow players. Even when playing on your own, it is important to get used to playing at the correct pitch.

Tuning device

You can simply use a tuning fork, or you can download an app. You don't need anything complicated. There are plenty available at no cost.

If you are going to invest in a metronome, then getting one with a tuner built in is even better.

Tuning Temperature

If the saxophone is *warm*, the pitch will be *higher* than if it is cold, so it is better to tune your instrument when it is warmed up. Rather than wait for this to happen gradually as you get playing, there is a quicker way:

Finger a bottom Bb so all the tone holes are covered. Breathe steadily through the instrument, air from the diaphragm. Push the air right through to the very end of the instrument whilst slackening off the embouchure so the reed does not vibrate and make a sound. This will produce a long huffing whisper down the instrument.

Tuning note

Now with the instrument warmed up, you can test your tuning note against your tuner. Tuning to a concert A is standard practice, so on alto and baritone sax you would play F# and on soprano and tenor sax you would play B (more on transposition in Chapter 23). Using the lower register for tuning will give you a more reliable guide, because it's less likely the pitch will waver with alterations in bottom lip pressure.

Length affects pitch

There are various ways you can alter the tuning, but first you need to check how far the mouthpiece is pushed onto the crook. Pushing the mouthpiece further onto the crook effectively makes the saxophone *shorter*, so this will make the pitch *higher*. Pulling the mouthpiece out makes the saxophone *longer*, so this will make the pitch *lower*.

Always ensure the crook cork is well greased so you can adjust the mouthpiece with ease. Move the mouthpiece forwards or backwards along the crook slightly until you find a pitch that matches your tuner.

Confident and true

When you test for tuning, always use a good solid tube of sound. Project the air through in a steady stream, breath level sustained by the diaphragm. Your tuning note needs to be played confidently. Playing tentatively can raise the pitch, and over blowing can lower the pitch. You should not have to tighten or slacken the embouchure to match up, just a default position sufficient to play an easy relaxed note is fine.

Maintaining pitch while playing

Your instrument is now correctly pitched, but as you get more proficient you'll notice some notes need tweaking to keep them in tune in relation to the rest of the instrument. Get in the habit of listening to your tuning during practice, and when playing with others. This is easiest to check when you come to any long notes within a phrase. Tighten the embouchure (*tennis net taut*), and you will *raise the pitch*, relax the embouchure (*tennis net slack*) and the *pitch will drop*. Players often refer to this as 'lipping up' or 'lipping down'.

Anticipating pitch

When you are just starting out, setting the position of the mouthpiece on the crook and keeping good control of air and embouchure will stand you in good stead. With experience you will start to automatically match your embouchure to an internalised sense of pitch. This is a very necessary skill that will develop naturally over time if you just listen and stay aware.

Hearing notes in your head before you play them brings about instinctive and involuntary subtle changes to the mouth cavity – changes that are needed to create the pitch you are aiming for. You can test this out by singing a low note and then a high note in your head and noticing how this feels. You may want to revisit Chapters 7 and 8 and remind yourself of the cherry, cathedral and the bullfrog.

A note about the tongue position.

Any references to tongue position earlier in this book have been deliberately unspecific. I know that by varying the position of the back of my tongue, I can maintain a round sound and adjust my pitch. This feels like a slow motion 'yaaa' type movement when opening out, and relaxing the 'yaaa' when adjusting back. This is particularly noticeable when playing with others because in an ensemble situation the pitch is never static, so it's a question of staying aware, listening and adapting all the time to blend in.

While players agree that keeping the throat open and relaxed is important, most say adjustments within the mouth have become so innate and automatic over time, they are unaware of the tongue position while playing. Some texts talk about 'flattening the back of the tongue' to help general sound production, particularly with the outer ranges of the instrument. This is where the concepts of cherry, cathedral and bull frog should help. It would be interesting to study MRI scans to gain some insight on the subject. Just getting into the habit of listening to your tone and tuning every time you play will develop your aural awareness. This will guide any subtle adjustments you'll need to make to tune in to others.

Meanwhile, here is something rather more tangible. A quick overview of your tuning check list:

Adjusting how far the mouthpiece is pushed along the crook

Maintaining air pressure

Lip tension

Jaw tension

Pitching and adjusting the back of the tongue

All instruments have their idiosyncrasies too, so knowing your instrument and which notes have a tendency to play slightly sharp or flat is part of the whole tuning experience. Of the four main saxophones, the soprano is the wildest beast to tame.

> *'The saxophone is an imperfect instrument, especially the tenor and soprano, as far as intonation goes. The challenge is to sing on an imperfect instrument that is outside of your body.'*
>
> **Stan Getz**

22

SQUEAKS
A SUBSTANTIAL LIST

Squeaks

With experience you get to recognise the different kind of squeaks.

Reed broken – never adjust the reed by pushing the tip/beware of catching it on clothing.

Reed worn out – if you've had it on for more than two weeks, try changing it, (Chapter 10 – acid).

Reed too soft – if you've been playing on the same strength reed for a while you may need to upgrade to a higher strength reed (Chapter 26).

Reed too hard – try dropping down a strength.

Reed too dry – take it off and give it a suck.

Reed in wrong position – check it is in line and that there is a finger nail of black at the top (Chapter 2).

Reed warped - Check the tip. If it's wrinkled then there are various solutions.

1. Popping the reed in a glass of water for 10 minutes.

2. With the reed in position, place your palm over the end of the mouthpiece and suck hard to create a vacuum, then without removing your hand, take your mouth away. The reed will stay stuck to the mouthpiece for a couple of seconds and then you will hear a resounding 'pop' as releases itself.

3. Place the reed on a clean surface flat side down. Press the sloped area down with your thumb fairly firmly, and draw the reed back slowly from under your finger. You may need to do this a few times to iron out any warping.

Mouth in wrong position – check skin of lip (Chapter 3).

Cheeks puffing – check in mirror – be sure that you are using the steamy window breath and have enough lip tension (bringing up slack on the tennis net). You may want to revisit Chapter 3.

Too much mouthpiece – edge the mouthpiece out a bit (Chapters 3 and 10).

Fingers catching keys – check the left index finger is not catching on the palm keys. Check that the right index finger is not catching on the side keys, (Chapter 5).

NB: *also check the trouble-shooting list, (Chapter 25).*

> *'I wanted to play saxophone, but all I could get were a few squeaks.'*
>
> **Stevie Ray Vaughan**

23

BASIC KEY AND TRANSPOSITION
AN UNDERSTANDING

The saxophone is a transposing instrument.

What does this mean?

Imagine there are six musicians in a room playing the following instruments:

Keyboard, violin, soprano sax, alto sax, tenor sax, baritone sax.

Everyone reads the note C.

The note you'll hear on *keyboard*, and *violin* is *C*.

The note you'll hear on *soprano and tenor* will be B^b, but the tenor will sound an octave lower.

The note you'll hear on *alto and baritone* will be E^b, but the baritone will sound an octave lower.

This is why saxophones are called B^b soprano sax, E^b alto sax, B^b tenor sax, E^b baritone sax.

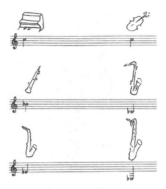

This means saxophones cannot play from the same music and sound the same as keyboard, violin or any other non-transposing instrument. Their music has to be adapted – transposed.

Within the saxophone family you will find that the same fingering will always correspond to the same written note, whichever one you play. This is just to simplify things rather than change fingerings between Eb and Bb instruments. You just need to remember the following:

Soprano and tenor can play the _same notes_ and sound the same as each other, but they will be an octave apart.

Alto and baritone can play the _same_ notes and sound the same as each other, but they will be an octave apart.

Soprano and alto cannot play the same notes and sound the same. Tenor and baritone cannot play the same notes and sound the same. For these instruments to match up, the music has to be transposed.

If you purchase music with keyboard accompaniment, it will be transposed for you, but further down the line it will be useful to learn how to do your own transpositions so you can play with others. If you do this often enough, the brain will find tricks and patterns to shortcut the process, enabling you to do the transposition in your head as you play. This is a really useful skill, but most people find they need to write parts out to feel secure.

The fingering for all four saxophones is the same, but the larger the instrument, the larger the mouthpiece. That means adapting embouchure accordingly. The larger you go, the more you slacken off the lips and jaw and the more you open out the tone chamber.

> 'I remember once, when I started writing for the alto saxophone, a saxophonist told me to think of it as being like a cross between an oboe and a viola, but louder.'

Gavin Bryars

24

CLEANING
STAYING TROUBLE FREE

Use a good quality pull through cleaning swab. Ones with cotton or chamois fabric work well. Avoid the felt variety because they don't absorb water. Use a bespoke saxophone pull through because it will be large enough to touch the tapering sides of the horn as it travels through, but not so large that it will get stuck inside the tube. The cord should have a weight at one end.

New learners may find cleaning the horn an awkward process to manage at the outset. Here is an easy way to feel secure handling the bulk of the instrument whilst avoiding getting the cloth jammed in the narrower section of the horn (a common occurrence).

Once you have taken the crook off the horn, rest the body of the instrument back on the sax case (see Chapter 2). Holding the narrower end of the horn with the left hand, drop the weighted end of the swab down the bell.

If you hold the cloth against the bell of the saxophone with the right hand, you will avoid the fabric getting bunched up.

Holding the swab against the bell of the horn

Now lift the bell end of the instrument with the right hand and tuck the horn under the left arm with the bell pointing towards the floor.

You will find that the weighted end just drops out of the neck of the horn

Weight drops out of neck

Holding the saxophone now with your left hand, the bulk of the instrument comfortably under your left arm, just draw the cord out of the horn and steadily away from you.

Crook

You will need a smaller swab for the crook. A cotton clarinet pull-through works really well because it won't scratch the inside of the tube. Just drop the weighted end through the larger opening of the tube and draw the swab through a couple of times.

Tenons

If you use your cotton clarinet swab to dry and gently polish the metal sleeve of the crook and the inside sleeve area of the narrower mouth of the horn (where metal touches metal), you will prevent dust and dirt collecting. This will ensure that the crook can always be pushed onto the horn without forcing.

Crook Cork

Keep the cork lubricated and it will be easier to push the mouthpiece onto the crook. Forcing can dislodge the octave mechanism. If the cork starts to dry out and the mouthpiece won't slide on easily, just use a dab of cork grease. You can work it in with your finger, but wash your hands afterwards if you are going to play, otherwise the grease ends up on the metalwork.

Mouthpiece

You can pull the cotton clarinet swab through the mouthpiece to keep it dry and clear of germs. Alternatively, you can just wipe the mouthpiece at either end with the cloth. If you do this, the tone chamber will not become worn with cleaning over time.

Every so often, you can give it a thorough clean. Fill a sink with **cold** water (avoid hot water as it will discolour the mouthpiece), and a tiny drop of washing up liquid. Gently clean with a soft toothbrush. Rinse with cold water, dry with a cloth and give it a spray with mouthpiece steriliser.

Reed

You can use the cotton material of your clarinet cleaner to dry off your reed. Sliding the reed back into its protective plastic case will stop it from getting damaged or warped.

Packing the saxophone in its case after each playing session will keep it protected from dust and dirt. Leaving the lid of the case open for ten minutes before closing it will enable the saxophone to dry out thoroughly.

NB: *If your saxophone came with a 'pad saver', then you can push it through the horn to clean it, but on no account leave it in the sax as the manufacturer intended. The moisture retained within the cleaner will create a continual damp atmosphere within the instrument and prevent the pads from drying properly. In fact, for this reason it's best to keep it out of the case entirely when packing away.*

25

TROUBLE SHOOTING AND MAINTENANCE

WHEN TO USE AN EXPERT

If you clean your saxophone thoroughly after playing, there should be few issues. However, here are some that students have experienced.

Notes not speaking, sounding weak or low notes bubbling

- One or more of the pads is not seated correctly over the hole.

- A pad is split and needs replacing.

- A key is bent and preventing a pad from covering its tone hole or else forcing a hole open that should be closed.

In all of these cases, take your saxophone to a technician.

Notes continuing in the upper register when octave key released

This is usually due to the octave mechanism not working correctly. The metal key on the crook is thin and vulnerable to bending when the crook is being handled, (see Chapter 2).

- If the key is bent the pad will no longer be covering the hole on the crook, in which case a quick tweak can sometimes solve the issue. Ask a teacher or technician to do this for you because you could end up with a broken key and an expensive repair job if you try and do this yourself.

- The horn to crook mechanism is forcing the octave key continuously open. Check you have the crook correctly aligned to the horn, (Chapter 2).

- Octave mechanism spring not functioning correctly. The spring should be strong enough to allow the pad to drop back onto its hole once the octave key has been released. If the spring is too weak or has been bent, then the pad will flop or bounce on the hole and top notes can pop out erratically which can be frustrating and annoying. It will need attention from a technician, but if you know a friendly sax player or have access to a teacher then they will be able to position an elastic band over the mechanism hold the key in place until you can get it properly repaired.

Problems sliding the crook onto the horn

Sliding the crook onto the horn should be easy, but oxide can build up on the sleeve of the horn opening and the tenon of the crook. Dust and dirt can also collect in these areas where metal touches metal.

If you ensure you dry the tenon on the crook and the inside of the top of the horn when you do your regular clean, you should not have a problem (Chapter 24).

Oxide has a greenish appearance and can be polished off with a dry cloth. Then rub on a very small amount of cork grease. If gunge collects, rubbing both areas with a dab of lighter fluid on a cotton cloth will clean it up nicely. If there is still a problem, trombone slide oil will get things moving. This is not an ideal solution, because the slide oil ultimately collects more dust and grime, so long term it will aggravate the problem. Using this as a quick fix is preferable to forcing the crook on or off, but if the issue persists, take it to your instrument technician. Never use metal polish to clean the sax.

Problems sliding the mouthpiece onto the crook

Keep the cork lubricated and it will be easy to slide the mouthpiece on and off. It is easy to dislodge or bend the octave mechanism if you have to force the mouthpiece on.

$G^\sharp$ not working

This is usually because the pad covering the $G^\sharp$ tone hole is sticky. Just slide the finger under the pad and flick the pad free.

Sticky Pads

Use a piece of plain paper – not too textured, printer paper would work: place one sheet between the pad and the hole it covers. Press down gently on the metal cup that holds the pad while drawing the paper out. This cleans off any sticky residue. If the problem persists, scribble some pencil lines on the paper and repeat the process.

Powder paper also works well. Woodwind specialists sell this in small packets, but face powder is just as effective and possibly cheaper. A more thorough clean can be achieved by rubbing the surface of the pad with a cotton wool bud dipped in lighter fluid.

Take care when cleaning the pads. The skins are delicate and if pierced or ripped will not maintain an airtight seal over the tone holes.

NB: *if you avoid eating or drinking before playing, then you will rarely have this problem. No sticky breath – cleaner pads.*

Save feasting till later

Swab jammed in horn

This is a common problem, but should be avoided if you use the method suggested in Chapter 2.

A gentle nudge on the blockage with a narrow blunt object like a chop stick from the neck end of the horn can sometimes dislodge it, but if the cleaner doesn't come free easily just take your sax to a teacher or technician. They will have seen this problem many times before and should be able to solve the problem quickly. It is easy to bend keys and push things out of adjustment by persisting. What was a simple issue can become an expensive repair job.

Servicing

As with a car, your saxophone will need to be serviced from time to time. You can take it to be serviced every six months, every year or every two years. This will depend upon how often you play just as how many miles you drive determines the regularity of your car service.

A full service will require taking all the keys off the saxophone and a thorough technician will normally clean away any grease, dust and dirt and give the body a polish.

Spring tension will be checked to ensure that the pads are held up or down sufficiently. The distance between the horn and pad cups will be balanced throughout the instrument so that the pads seal correctly on the holes.

The state of the pads will be checked. These need to be in good order so they create an airtight seal when in place over the tone holes. Split and worn pads will need to be replaced.

Finally, the mechanism will be lubricated to keep all parts moving smoothly.

Keep your sax in tip-top condition, and it will serve you well.

NB: *Your saxophone needs to be set up to be ergonomically manageable for you. If the keys feel high under the fingers or the keywork feels heavy to operate, have a discussion with your technician. The tension on the springs can be adjusted and loosened throughout the whole mechanism, or on just the odd key as needed. This may be something you discuss when purchasing your instrument as part of your set up requirements (see Chapter 1).*

26

MOUTHPIECE, LIGATURE AND REED

KEEP IT SIMPLE

Mouthpiece

You may have a top of the range saxophone, but it will still be difficult to make a good sound if you have an inferior mouthpiece. By contrast,a basic student saxophone can make a good sound if you have a good mouthpiece.

There are many mouthpieces on the market to choose from, with varying characteristics, but it is best to keep simple when you first start out.

A Yamaha 4C is an excellent, inexpensive starter mouthpiece. You can always upgrade when you have gained enough technical control to notice the difference in tone, and enough listening experience to know what sound you want to create.

Ligature

The type of ligature you choose can also make a difference to your tone, but as with the mouthpiece, it's best to keep your choices simple and functional until your playing has progressed enough to appreciate a real difference.

A standard metal ligature with screws at the front is fine – but beware, some cheap quality metal ones can keep sliding off the mouthpiece, dislodging the reed. Be sure your ligature will hold in place as you tighten the screws. The fabric or leather type with the screw at the back is slightly easier to set up. If you go for a leather ligature, then choose a thicker, more robust type. It will hold its shape better and continue to support the reed on the mouthpiece. BG leather ligatures maintain their grip well.

Reed

The lip muscles will be weaker and under-developed when you first start playing the saxophone, so you need a reed which will vibrate easily with little resistance.

Reeds come in different densities, the higher the number, the denser the reed. There are many brands on the market and many styles to choose from. Costs vary, but a poor quality reed will never give you a good sound. When purchasing a reed, you need to consider the cut. There are two types, American and French and you need to find which will work best with your mouthpiece.

Here are a couple of suggested brands and strengths for beginners.

American Cut:

Rico Reeds (orange box). Strength 1.5 or 2 is a good starting place. As you venture into the upper register and your lip muscles firm up, you can then progress up to a 2.5 strength.

French Cut:

Vandoren reeds (there are many types, but stick with traditional for starters). Strength 1 or 1.5, moving to 2 or 2.5 as muscles firm.

Once you have gained control of the upper register, keep assessing the sound you make. If you wish, you can then experiment with a denser reed, but take your time. It does not necessarily follow that the more experienced the player, the greater the strength of reed. There are many professionals who find they can get the flexibility, resonance and roundness of tone they need on a softer reed.

Comfort and physicality play a part, too. As with ligature and mouthpiece, reed choice is very much a personal preference. These are all aspects to consider further down the line as you tweak your 'unique saxophone voice'.

27

ACCESSORIES
THE ONES YOU NEED

As with any new hobby, there are so many accessories out there to tempt you. Best not over-spend until you have been playing a while and know what you will really need. However, generally speaking, it's better to spend rather more for a good quality product to ensure it will do the job properly.

Useful accessories that really make a difference:

Saxophone pull through: Essential for cleaning. Get a good quality one designed specifically for the saxophone, (see chapter 24). For the soprano, a good quality oboe pull through does the job well. Many oboists use a peacock feather. This will also work on soprano sax if you have access to an altruistic peacock.

Clarinet pull through: This is exactly the right size for pulling through the crook. Stick to cotton rather than felt and you can also use it to dry the reed.

Mouthpiece sterilizer: Prevents germs collecting in the mouthpiece.

Cork grease: Essential for keeping the cork on the crook lubricated so that the mouthpiece will screw on easily.

Mouthpiece patch: This is a rubber pad that sticks onto the top of the mouthpiece. It absorbs some of the vibration which makes playing more comfortable – the teeth feel as if they are sitting on a cushion. Worth paying a bit more for the thicker variety so you can really tell the difference.

Sling: There is a variety to choose from. If you are playing baritone sax or have a tendency towards back problems you may prefer the harness type that you clip yourself into. This allows the weight of the saxophone to be spread across the length of your back, rather than across your neck.

Sax stand: Keep the sax on a stand and you'll pick it up and play more regularly. Bell size can vary, particularly in the case of vintage saxes, so if you are playing on an older sax it's a good idea to take it with you when choosing which stand to buy just to be sure that it fits. The tenor requires slightly more length between the restraints than the alto, but many sax stands nowadays will adapt to either fitting. There is a collapsible design that stores in the bell, which is handy if you are regularly out and about with your playing.

Music stand: It is good practice to rest your music on a stand. It will avoid you straining your neck to read at an angle, and it will improve your playing position.

Palm risers: These inexpensive flexible rubber sleeves usually come in a small pack. They can be pushed onto the palm keys to raise the position slightly which can make it easier to move around the higher notes.

Mute: There are a variety of mutes on the market, and there is some controversy as to how effective they are. As the sound escapes from the tone holes down the entire length of the saxophone, the only way to substantially mute the sound is to enclose the instrument entirely. There is a pricey device on the market that actually does do this, but operating the weighty structure seems akin to using a laboratory glove box!

'I wanted an electric train for Christmas but I got the saxophone instead.'

Clarence Clemons

28

BACK PAGE

READING FROM THE END BACKWARDS

It is an odd fact that mistakes often happen towards the end of a piece of music. Here are some possible reasons why.

Typical practice habit

Most people start at the beginning (an obvious place to start). They go wrong, start again, go wrong, start again, etc, etc, etc.

The end of the piece rarely gets played

The beginning gets played many times, but the end of the piece rarely gets reached—so that section doesn't get played very often - it's not very familiar.

Concentration diminishes

Most people are more alert at the beginning of a task. We take for granted the simultaneous skill of reading music with the coordination involved in playing an instrument. This requires a huge amount of concentration.

Anxiety increases

As you venture into uncharted territory, the likelihood of going wrong is greater.

Solution:

Start your practice session with the end of the piece.

THE END

ABOUT THE AUTHOR

Louise graduated from the London College of Music with ALCM and LLCM and began her first post as Woodwind teacher for North Devon LEA. Since her subsequent post as Woodwind tutor for Blundell's School, Louise's ongoing freelance work in Somerset has involved teaching people of all ages and performing with a variety of Classical, Jazz and Klezmer ensembles.

Her music projects have been many and varied. They include co-founding *The High Park Community Music School,* which enables any child to play music; forming the adult band *Hoot* moving adults towards improvisation; and collaborating on *The Mosaic of Art and Vision,* workshops designed to teach children how to create art inspired by music.

Since gaining a B Sc (Hons) in Psychology, Louise has focussed attention on the hurdles that limit playing potential and developing *Wizwind.* This innovative and compelling teaching method is designed for people who struggle to read music, enabling students to choose a tune one week and be playing it the next. The *Wizwind* method liberates students whose reliance on reading music prevents them from developing their improvising potential.

During Covid, when restrictions have allowed, fellow musicians have trekked to rehearse in a large barn where Louise lives on a remote farm, warmed by a fire pit and overlooking fields of bemused cattle.

The Self-Taught Sax Player was inspired by a realisation that not everyone is so lucky. Some insights from a friendly musician who has 'done her time in the cells' (as music students term it) might encourage and spur on the lonely blower at this challenging time.

Louise's other woodwind titles in this series, *The Lockdown Clarinettist* and *The Self-Taught Flute Player* are also available.

Look out for further Wizwind inspirations coming your way soon!

Made in United States
Orlando, FL
18 May 2022

17957626R00063